American Symbols
AND THEIR Meanings

THE
LIBERTY
BELL

American Symbols AND THEIR Meanings

THE LIBERTY BELL

HAL MARCOVITZ

MASON CREST PUBLISHERS
PHILADELPHIA

Produced by OTTN Publishing, Stockton, N.J.

Mason Crest Publishers
370 Reed Road
Broomall PA 19008
www.masoncrest.com

3 5 7 9 8 6 4

Library of Congress Cataloging-in-Publication Data

Marcovitz, Hal.
  The Liberty Bell / Hal Marcovitz.
      p. cm. — (American symbols and their meanings)
Summary: Traces the history of the Liberty Bell, including information about the use of bells in colonial America, statistics about this particular bell, legends surrounding it, and its importance as an American symbol.
  Includes bibliographical references and index.
  ISBN 1-59084-025-9
1. Liberty Bell—Juvenile literature. 2. Philadelphia (Pa.)—Buildings, structures, etc.—Juvenile literature.
[1. Liberty Bell.   2. Bells—History.]
I. Title. II. Series.
F158.8.I3M374 2003
973.3—dc21
                                                    2002009580

American Symbols
AND THEIR Meanings

CONTENTS

The Importance of American Symbols

Symbols are not merely ornaments to admire—they also tell us stories. If you look at one of them closely, you may want to find out why it was made and what it truly means. If you ask people who live in the society in which the symbol exists, you will learn some things. But by studying the people who created that symbol and the reasons why they made it, you will understand the deepest meanings of that symbol.

The United States owes its identity to great events in history, and the most remarkable American Symbols are rooted in these events. The struggle for independence from Great Britain gave America the Declaration of Independence, the Liberty Bell, the American flag, and other images of freedom. The War of 1812 gave the young country a song dedicated to the flag, "The Star-Spangled Banner," which became our national anthem. Nature gave the country its national animal, the bald eagle. These symbols established the identity of the new nation, and set it apart from the nations of the Old World.

To be emotionally moving, a symbol must strike people with a sense of power and unity. But it often takes a long time for a new symbol to be accepted by all the people, especially if there are older symbols that have gradually lost popularity. For example, the image of Uncle Sam has replaced Brother Jonathan, an earlier representation of the national will, while the Statue of Liberty has replaced Columbia, a woman who represented liberty to Americans in the early 19th century. Since then, Uncle Sam and the Statue of Liberty have endured and have become cherished icons of America.

Of all the symbols, the Statue of Liberty has perhaps the most curious story, for unlike other symbols, Americans did not create her. She was created by the French, who then gave her to America. Hence, she represented not what Americans thought of their country but rather what the French thought of America. It was many years before Americans decided to accept this French goddess of Liberty as a symbol for the United States and its special role among the nations: to spread freedom and enlighten the world.

This series of books is valuable because it presents the story of each of America's great symbols in a freshly written way and will contribute to the students' knowledge and awareness of them. It is to be hoped that this information will awaken an abiding interest in American history, as well as in the meanings of American symbols.

—*Barry Moreno,*
librarian and historian
Ellis Island/Statue of Liberty National Monument

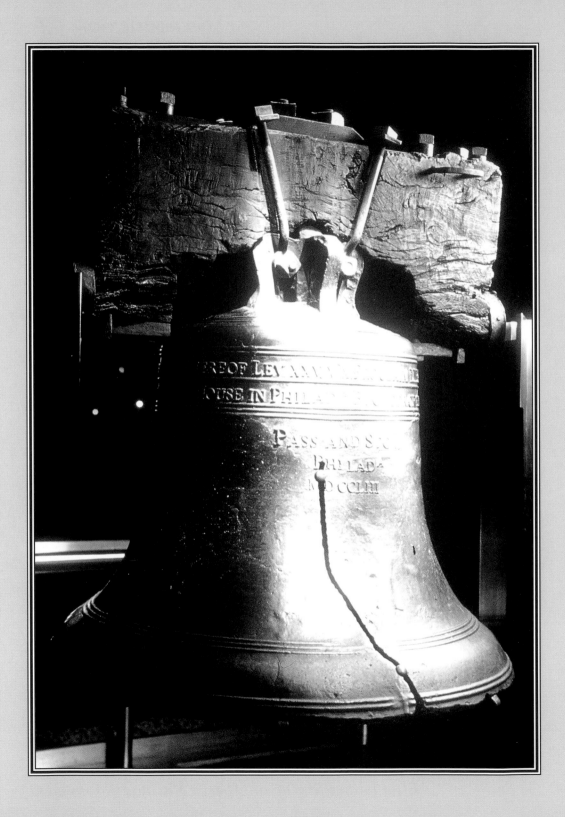

The bell that would become one of the great American symbols of freedom and democracy was nearly destroyed by the British during the American Revolution. A group of farmers moved the bell from Philadelphia to a town in the country, where it was hidden. Had the British found the bell, it might have been melted down into musket balls that would be fired at the Continental Army.

A Narrow Escape

In September 1777, at the height of America's War for Independence, farmers Frederick Leaser and John Jacob Mickley drove their wagons some 50 miles from their Lehigh Valley farms to Philadelphia, the capital city of the new nation. They had been summoned to help remove 11 bells from the city that military and civilian leaders feared would be captured by the British and melted down to make *ammunition*.

By the time Leaser, Mickley, and 200 other farmers arrived in Philadelphia, the Revolutionary War was not going well for the colonists. After early British defeats at Concord and Bunker Hill, the two sides had battled hard, each scoring victories. But by August 1777, a force of British soldiers under General William Howe was advancing on Philadelphia. Howe planned to capture the capital with his soldiers and cut off the city's harbor on the Delaware River with ships from the British navy. American troops **skirmished** with Howe's men at the battles of Brandywine and Paoli, but were unable to turn back the Redcoats.

As Howe's men approached Philadelphia, nearly everyone in town helped prepare the capital for the British occupation. First, the Continental Congress moved out of the city to Lancaster, about 100 miles away, so the government could continue during the occupation. Next, the **Assembly** of Pennsylvania—the state's government—convened on September 14, 1777, at the State House on Chestnut Street in Philadelphia, and issued this order:

> That Colonel Benjamin Flower employ James Worrell, Francis Allison and Mr. Evans, carpenters, or such other workmen as he may think proper to employ, to take down the bells of all the public buildings in this city and convey them to safety.

The four men had their work cut out for them. Many of the bells were hung high in church **steeples**; others were very heavy. In fact, the men started their work right at the State House where a grand bell hung in the tower. This bell weighed 2,080 pounds and had been hanging in the State House since 1753. It had chimed to announce many of the great events of the time. The bell was seen as an important symbol during the early years of the new nation. The inscription on the bell promised it would "Proclaim *Liberty* throughout all the Land."

But it would never ring for liberty again if the British captured the bell and melted it down for bullets.

Flower and his helpers removed the bell from the State House, as well as the other 10 bells they found around the city. Their work did not go unnoticed by the citizens of the capital. On September 22, 1777, Philadelphian Elizabeth Drinker wrote in her diary: "All ye bells in ye city are certainly taken away and there is also talk of pump handles and fire buckets being taken also, but that may be only conjecture. Things seem to be, upon ye whole drawing towards great confusion. May we be strengthened in the time of trial."

The bell from the State House was hoisted into the wagon driven by Mickley. He joined a train of other wagons that left the city and headed north. By the time General Howe and 3,000 British troops marched into Philadelphia on September 27, all the bells in the city were gone.

The wagon train under Flower's command made its way through the countryside. The road was rough, and the bell in Mickley's wagon bumped along as the huge wooden wheels rolled in and out of dry, rocky ruts as

> **When struck, the Liberty Bell will play the E-flat note.**

well as slick, muddy flats. Along the way, the wagons containing the bells met up with some 700 army wagons also heading north. Finally, the wagons arrived in Bethlehem, known then as Northamptontowne. At the time, the town had fewer than 40 homes. Flower quickly concluded there was no good place in town to hide 11 very large and heavy bells. He decided to continue the journey to nearby Allentown. While heading for Allentown, though, Mickley's wagon broke down. The train stopped, and the great State House bell was moved to the wagon driven by Frederick Leaser.

Flower found places in Allentown to hide all 11 bells. On the morning of September 25, 1777, the bell from the State House was hidden in the basement of the Zion High German Reformed Church. Flower's men pried up the floorboards so they could lower the bell into the basement.

Although the British did occupy Philadelphia, they left in 1779 to continue fighting the war elsewhere. The bell at Zion church was returned to the steeple of the State House. Years later, the State House in Philadelphia would become known as Independence Hall, and the bell hanging in its steeple would earn the name Liberty Bell.

In later years, the government of Pennsylvania erected tablets *commemorating* the roles Mickley and Leaser played in saving the State House bell from the hands of the British.

Mickley's tablet was placed outside the church in

Lehigh Valley farmers Frederick Leaser and John Jacob Mickley answered the call to duty in Philadelphia in 1777, where they helped hide the city's bells from the advancing British army, which intended to melt them down for bullets. The bell from the Pennsylvania State House was first loaded into Mickley's wagon, but when the wagon broke down on the way to Allentown, the bell was transferred to Leaser's wagon.

Leaser (whose name is also found to be spelled Loeser, Liesser, and Leiser) was born in 1738. He was the father of seven children, and farmed in Lynn Township, Northampton County. At the age of 19, Leaser enlisted in the Colonial Army and fought in the French and Indian War. Later, he enlisted as a private in the Continental Army and fought in the American Revolution.

Mickley was a farmer in Whitehall Township, Northampton County. He held a number of positions in his local government, serving as a member of his township's General Committee, which set the laws for his community.

Allentown, which still stands today and is now known as Zion's Reformed United Church of Christ. The tablet reads: "In commemoration of the saving of the Liberty Bell from the British in September 1777. Erected to the memory of John Jacob Mickley, member of the General Committee from Whitehall Township, Northampton County, Pennsylvania, who, under the cover of darkness, and with his farm team hauled the Liberty Bell from Independence Hall, Philadelphia, through the British lines to Bethlehem."

A group of men dressed in Revolution-era uniforms parades outside Independence Hall in Philadelphia. The building was constructed during the 1730s as a meeting place for the state's lawmakers. In 1752 the tall bell tower was added, and a special bell was ordered. This bell would be used to announce important events in the colony.

TO PROCLAIM LIBERTY

In October 1728, the Assembly of Pennsylvania set aside money to build a meeting place for the colony's legislators. The building was finished in 1736. Fifteen years later, the legislators voted to add a bell tower to the south side of what had become known as the State House. The tower was completed in 1752.

In colonial America, bells were a very important method of communication. When citizens heard the *peal* of a bell, they knew to gather in a public square to hear important announcements. The sound of bells could provide information. A muffled tone meant a *solemn* message—possibly the death of an important person.

Fast rings meant a fire had started somewhere in the city, and citizens knew to bring their buckets to the square. Bells would chime at six o'clock in the morning to rouse people from their beds; at noon, to announce the midday meal; and at nine o'clock at night, to advise citizens to leave the streets because the *curfew* had arrived. Nine rings of the bell had a special meaning— the chimes announced the death of an unfortunate convict, hanged in the public square.

And so, the assembly decided it needed a bell suitable and fitting to ring in the important news and events for what was, at the time, America's greatest city.

Isaac Norris, the speaker of the Pennsylvania Assembly who headed the effort to obtain a bell for the steeple of the State House, was the son of a wealthy merchant who arrived in Philadelphia in 1692. Isaac Norris was raised as a member of the Society of Friends, the religious group known as the Quakers. Young Isaac was educated for a time in England. By the time he returned to join the family business he was fluent in Hebrew, Latin, and French.

When Norris's father died, Isaac took over the family business and prospered. He became active in the government of the province of Pennsylvania, becoming a member in 1736 and speaker in 1750. Norris believed strongly in civil rights and felt the American colonies should be free. In 1751 he instructed the bell's foundry to inscribe the bell with these words: "Proclaim Liberty throughout all the Land unto all the Inhabitants thereof."

Norris would not live long enough to see independence. He became ill in 1764 and resigned from the assembly. He died in 1766.

On November 1, 1751, with construction of the bell tower under way, Assembly Speaker Isaac Norris wrote to Robert Charles in England, asking Charles to find a foundry to make the State House bell. As speaker, Norris had been elected by the other assembly members to head the legislature. He was responsible for setting the *agenda* of the government, deciding which issues should be taken up by the members, and seeing to various administrative duties. Charles was the representative in London for Pennsylvania's interests, responsible for communications between the colony and the king.

In his letter, Norris asked Charles "to get us a good bell of about two thousand pounds weight." He also gave these instructions to Charles:

> We hope and rely on thy care and assistance in this affair and that thou wilt procure and forward it by the first good opportunity as our workmen inform us it will be much less trouble to hang the bell before their scaffolds are struck from the building where we intend to place it which will not be done 'till the end of next summer or beginning of the fall. Let the bell be cast by the best workmen and examined carefully before it is shipped with the following words well shaped in large letters round it: "By order of the Assembly of the *Province* of [Pennsylvania] for the Statehouse in the City of Philadelphia, 1752." And underneath, "Proclaim Liberty throughout all the Land unto all the Inhabitants Thereof — Levit. XXV 10."

To "Proclaim Liberty throughout all the Land . . ."

It was a bold *prophecy,* for at the time Pennsylvania,

like the other American colonies, was firmly under the iron grip of the king of England. In the years to follow, fervor for revolution would brew in the colonies, leading up to 1776, when the Continental Congress, meeting in the State House in Philadelphia, would declare America's independence from Great Britain.

The founder of Pennsylvania, William Penn's desire for freedom clearly influenced Isaac Norris as well as other members of the Pennsylvania Assembly who sought a bell to proclaim liberty throughout their land.

He was born in 1644 in London. While attending school, Penn became a member of the Society of Friends. Friends were known as Quakers, because they were said to "quake" while listening to the voice of God.

Quakers found religious intolerance in England. Many were imprisoned, including Penn. In 1681, Penn obtained a grant of land in the New World from the king of England in repayment of a debt owed his father. A year later, he arrived in the New World and established a colony for Quakers under the name Pennsylvania, which in Latin means "Penn's Woods." He planned and named the city of Philadelphia, which in Greek means Brotherly Love. One of his greatest accomplishments was the writing of the "Charter of Privileges," which granted religious freedom to all the people living in the colony.

Penn returned to England to aid Quakers who were still persecuted there. He died in England in 1718.

It is likely, though, that Norris was not looking that far ahead when he selected the inscription for the bell. Instead, it is believed that he chose the verse from the Biblical book of Leviticus to celebrate the 50th anniversary of the "Charter of Privileges" that had been drawn up by William Penn, founder of the colony. On October 28, 1701, Penn wrote the charter, which became the law of Pennsylvania. Among the provisions of Penn's charter was establishment of an elected assembly to govern the colony of Pennsylvania.

Leviticus verse 10, chapter 25, reads:

"And ye shall hallow the fiftieth year, and proclaim liberty throughout all the land unto the inhabitants thereof: it shall be a jubilee unto you; and ye shall return every man unto his possession, and ye shall return every man unto his family."

Norris decided to buy the bell from an English *foundry* because, at the time, there were few foundries in America capable of producing such a massive bell. There were blacksmiths and craftsmen who worked with metal in every city and village, but most people were farmers.

Charles decided to order the bell from Thomas Lester, master founder at the Whitechapel Bell Foundry. Lester began by fashioning a solid core that would serve as a mold for the bell; he composed the core from a mixture of clay, horse manure, and cow hair that was shaped into a rough form of the bell. The core was heated over a fire until it hardened. Next, he applied another layer of clay, this time including the details that would be found in the final version—the lettering and raised decorative lines. Again, the bell mold was heated over a fire until hard.

That version of the mold was greased with animal fat, and then another layer of clay was applied to make a hollow mold. After that mold was heated and hardened, it was broken off in sections and reassembled.

Now, Lester had a hollow mold of the bell. His next step was to pour the bubbling-hot, liquefied bell metal into the mold. Lester used mostly copper and tin for the bell. The *cast* bell was allowed to cool several days. Finally, the bell could be lifted out of its mold.

Back in the colonies, Norris and the other assembly members anxiously awaited the bell's completion. "We are looking for the bell daily," Norris wrote to Charles.

The wait ended in September 1752 when the British ship *Myrtilla* sailed up the Delaware River, arriving at the port of

All bells share four main common parts. They include the sound bow, which is the thick lower lip of the bell and the widest part of the bell; the waist, which is the *concave* portion of the bell that curves in and up toward the top; the shoulder, which rises above the waist and begins the curve of the bell in toward the top; and the crown, which caps off the bell. Other parts of the bell are the cannons, which are the loops cast into the crown that enables the bell to hang from a wooden yolk, and the clapper, a hammer that hangs inside the bell and makes the ringing sound as it strikes against the bell's walls while the bell swings.

Philadelphia. The bell was unloaded from the *Myrtilla* and driven by horse and wagon to the courtyard of the State House, where it was set up until it could be

> **Pennsylvania is misspelled on the Liberty Bell; on the bell, Isaac Norris directed the name of the future state spelled "Pensylvania."**

hoisted aloft into the tall bell tower.

Why not a test? Somebody in the courtyard—history does not record who—drew the *clapper* back and let it swing. The vibrations caused by the first strike of the clapper tore a crack into the new bell.

"I had the mortification to hear that it was cracked by the stroke of the clapper without any other [violence] as it was hung up to try the sound," Norris wrote to Charles. The assembly speaker wanted the bell shipped back to England for repairs at Whitechapel. "Our judges have generally agreed the metal was too high and brittle," he wrote.

Bell maker Thomas Lester became quite angry when he learned that Norris blamed him for the crack in the bell. Lester argued that there was nothing wrong with the mix of the metals or the workmanship. Instead, he blamed the crack on an "amateur bell ringer."

Norris and the other assembly members soon found they could not immediately return the bell to Whitechapel for repairs. The *Myrtilla*, soon to sail for England, had already been loaded with cargo and had no room for the bell. Norris was forced to find somebody else to repair the bell. They didn't have to look far. Just a few blocks from the State House, a foundry operated by John Pass and John Stow had opened just six months before.

Stow had learned metalworking in England while Pass had immigrated to America from Malta, a British-occupied island in the Mediterranean Sea between Africa and Italy. Pass and Stow specialized in brass work, making small kitchen gadgets and tools. The only bells a customer might find for sale in their shop were the small bells a citizen might hang outside the front door, or to place on a wagon to jingle as the horse trotted along a country road. Nevertheless, Pass and Stow assured Norris they were capable of recasting the huge bell, and Norris soon agreed to let them take on the job.

Pass and Stow smashed the bell with hammers until it was broken into pieces. Then they melted these down. They probably made their molds for the bell in the same way Lester had at Whitechapel, because Stow had learned to operate a foundry in England. However, Pass and Stow did tinker with the recipe. They poured in more copper and added about 190 pounds to the overall weight of the bell.

Norris kept a watchful eye on the work. On March 10, 1753, he wrote to Charles in England: "I am just now informed that they have opened the mould, and have got a good bell, which I confess pleases me very much that we should first venture upon and succeed in the greatest bell cast, for ought I know, in English America.

The mould was finished in a very masterly manner and the letters, I am told, are better than in the old one."

A few weeks later, the bell was finished. The main differences between the two versions were the addition of the words "Pass and Stow," an abbreviation for Philadelphia, and the date 1753 in Roman numerals molded into the waist of the bell.

Woolley and his men hoisted the new bell aloft into the steeple of the State House and in April, the great bell issued its first chimes. But those who heard the bell

Isaac Norris, the speaker of the Pennsylvania Assembly, called John Pass and John Stow "two ingenious work-men" capable of re-casting the bell, which had cracked soon after its arrival from England.

They had opened their metalworking business just a few months before the bell's arrival in America in 1752, specializing in producing tools and small gadgets.

John Stow was born in Philadelphia on February 2, 1727, the second son of Charles and Rebecca Stow. He learned to work a foundry in England. In Philadelphia, he was a charter member of the Union Library Company. Stow died in March 1754, the year following the final casting of the bell.

John Pass was a native of the British island of Malta and may have served as an apprentice bell founder there. After leaving Malta, Pass owned Mount Holly Iron Furnace in New Jersey before arriving in Philadelphia. John Pass probably did not know how to read or write; on the bill submitted to the assembly for payment for delivering the bell, John Stow wrote his name but John Pass made the mark of an "X."

The State House bell is tested in the Pass and Stow Foundry. Among those pictured here are the colonial statesman, writer, and scientist Benjamin Franklin (third from left).

hardly described the sound as a "chime." Instead, the sound was described as more of a dull thud.

Once again, Norris found himself writing to Robert Charles in England, reporting a failure in the matter of the State House bell. "They made the mould in a masterly manner and run the metal well, but upon [trial], it seems they added too much copper in the present bell which is now hung up in its place," he wrote.

The bell came down from its loft and returned to Pass and Stow for still another recast. Again, Pass and Stow changed the mixture of the metals, hoping for a more *melodic* sound. The third version was completed in June

1753, and raised into the steeple of the State House. The newspaper *Pennsylvania Gazette* reported the event:

> Last week was raised and [fixed] in the Statehouse steeple the new great bell, cast here by Pass and Stow, weighing 2,080 pounds with this motto, Proclaim Liberty throughout all the Land unto all inhabitants thereof; Leviticus, XXV 10.

Norris was still not happy with the sound. The assembly speaker ordered still another bell purchased from England. It was delivered in 1754, but by then the assembly believed it was too much trouble to hoist the new bell aloft to replace the old bell. After all, the bell had been in use now for about a year.

And so the Pass and Stow version was permitted to remain in the steeple. Over the years, the people of Philadelphia came to refer to the Pass and Stow bell in the tower as the "Old One," while the newer bell was hung from a turret in the State House below the tower.

The Pass and Stow bell remained in the steeple of the State House for the next 24 years until it was taken down and hidden from the Redcoats. In that time, the

> The newer bell eventually ended up in a nearby church that burned down in 1844. The bell was severely damaged in the fire. The metal was melted down and recast into another bell, which eventually found a home at a nearby college.

bell became a symbol for the American people that would, indeed, proclaim liberty throughout all the land.

The crack in the Liberty Bell is clearly visible in this photograph of the bell. Over the years, the bell has suffered other damage as well. People have chipped away the edges of the bell as souvenirs. Though today the Liberty Bell is famous for its crack, no one knows for certain how or when the bell was originally broken.

THE CRACK IN THE LIBERTY BELL

On July 8, 1835, the great bell in the tower of the old Pennsylvania State House—now known as Independence Hall—announced the death of John Marshall, the chief justice of the United States. Although there is some evidence to the contrary, it is believed that was the day the Liberty Bell acquired its famous crack.

For several decades after the bell was hung in the State House in 1753, it was used as the Assembly of Pennsylvania had intended: to chime when there was news of important events and to call people to the public square to hear announcements.

On July 6, 1835, Marshall died while visiting

Philadelphia. For two days, the bell in Independence Hall chimed slowly while a funeral procession was prepared to transport his body back to his native Virginia. On July 8, the bell cracked.

Or did it?

If it did crack on that day, nobody bothered to make note of it. In fact, there is evidence to suggest the bell might have picked up its crack much earlier. For example, newspaper accounts reporting the visit of the Marquis de Lafayette to Philadelphia in September 1824 do not make mention of the ringing of the old bell. It should have been a festive occasion—the marquis was a French military hero who had helped lead the American troops during the Revolution. Certainly, his presence

John Marshall (1755–1835) was an important early American leader. After serving as a captain in the Continental Army during the revolution, he studied law. He was elected to the Virginia legislature, where he helped persuade the legislature to ratify the U.S. Constitution. After serving as minister to France and as secretary of state under president John Adams, Marshall was sworn in as the fourth chief justice of the United States Supreme Court. The decisions he made during his 34 years on the court still influence the way the U.S. government operates.

When the American Revolution began, the Marquis de Lafayette, a young French nobleman, came to America to fight on the side of the colonists. He earned his greatest glory during the successful Yorktown campaign in 1781, which led to the end of the war. Afterward, Lafayette went back to France, where he participated in the French Revolution. When he returned to the United States in 1824, he was given a hero's welcome by cheering crowds in many cities.

would have prompted the ringing of the city's greatest bell—unless, of course, the bell was cracked and could not be rung.

In 1828, the bell was rung to announce the news of the passage of the Catholic Emancipation Act of 1828 in Great Britain. Author John Sartain, in his book, *Reminiscences of a Very Old Man*, claimed the bell was cracked at this time. He wrote:

> The final passage of the Emancipation Act by the British Parliament is linked to a bit of Philadelphia history. On receipt of the news in Philadelphia the Liberty Bell in the tower of the State House was rung, and cracked in the ringing. When I was up in the tower in 1830, two years after, viewing the cracked bell for the first time, Downing, who was then the custodian of Independence Hall, told me of it and remarked that the bell refused to ring for a British Act, even when the Act was a good one.

If the bell cracked in 1828, the damage was not severe enough to limit its use. In 1831, Philadelphia City Council passed a resolution allowing all young men in the city to ring the bell on July 4. Additionally, the newspaper *National Gazette and Literary Register* reported that the bell would be rung at this time, and city fire fighters should not mistake it for the fire bell.

There is documentation that the bell rang on February 22, 1832, to honor the birthday of George Washington. And then, on November 14 of that year, the bell rang again to announce the death of the last living signer of the Declaration of Independence, Charles Carroll. Two years later, the bell was tolled to announce the death of the Marquis de Lafayette.

A Philadelphian named Emmanuel Joseph Rauch claimed to have been responsible for making the crack.

During the early years of the 19th century, the State House bell was often rung on George Washington's birthday. Did the Liberty Bell crack while being tolled to honor the first president of the United States?

In a letter to the *New York Times* in 1911, Rauch said that as a boy, he was passing by Independence Hall on February 22, 1835, when the steeple keeper asked if he would like to ring the Liberty Bell in honor of George Washington's birthday. The steeple keeper took Emmanuel and several other boys up to the tower and showed them how to ring the bell. The boys pulled the rope and noticed a change in the tone of the bell.

"On the side of the bell that hung toward Walnut Street, we found that there was a big crack, a foot or fifteen inches long," Rauch said. "What happened after that I forget: boy-like, I didn't do any worrying and heard no more about the cracking of the bell until some years later. Then, however, and many times since, I have read of how the bell came to be cracked, but never have I seen the version which I have just given."

> In 1915, the Franklin Institute in Philadelphia determined the cause of the crack was the two re-castings performed by Pass and Stow in 1753. Heating and re-heating metals causes them to lose their strength over time, making them as "brittle as glass," the Franklin Institute said. In addition to the larger crack, the Institute also found a a hairline crack through the names Pass and Stow on the bell.

If the bell did crack during Marshall's funeral in 1835, the superintendents of Independence Hall clearly believed the crack was not serious enough to render the bell useless. Indeed, the bell would ring again in coming years, but each time the crack would grow.

The crack in the bell begins between the P and H in the abbreviation for Philadelphia, then heads down to the lip. Workers tried to repair the crack. File marks are clearly visible along the sides of the crack, but their efforts obviously failed.

The bell was rung during the viewing of the body of deceased President William Henry Harrison on April 7, 1841, and to celebrate Washington's birthday on February 22, 1843. It was probably tolled for the last time on Washington's birthday in 1846. Any sounds the bell has made since then have been produced with a rubber mallet struck carefully against its side.

Here is how the *Philadelphia Public Ledger* newspaper reported the last tolling of the Liberty Bell, in a story published February 26, 1846:

> The old Independence Bell rang its last clear note on Monday last in honor of the birthday of Washington and now hangs in the great city steeple irreparably cracked and dumb. It had been cracked before but was set in order that day by having the edges of the fracture filed so as not to vibrate against each other. It gave out clear notes and loud, and appeared to be in excellent condition until noon, when it received a sort of compound fracture in a zigzag direction through one of its sides which put it completely out of tune and left it a mere wreck of what it was.

In 1852, the bell came down from the steeple and was placed on a pedestal in front of Independence Hall. It made many trips in the coming years; it was transported

During the second half of the 19th century, the Liberty Bell made many trips around the country. This photograph was taken while the bell was passing through Plainfield, Connecticut, in June 1903. The Liberty Bell was on its way to Boston for a celebration of the battle of Bunker Hill.

to expositions and fairs and riding atop floats in parades. In May 1919, the bell was taken out of Independence Hall so that it could be displayed for a military parade honoring the troops returning from World War I. After this, however, the bell's *caretakers* concluded that any future movement of the bell would severely damage America's chief symbol of freedom and democracy. The bell was placed back on its pedestal inside Independence Hall, where it remained for the next 57 years.

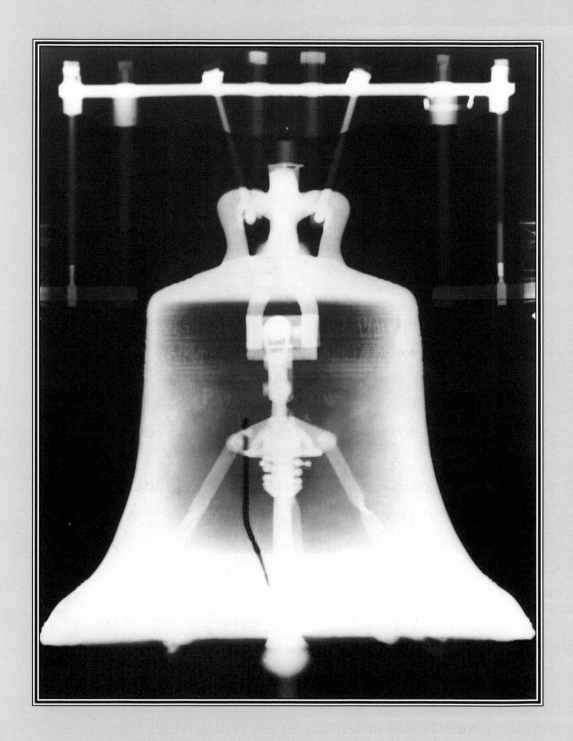

There are more cracks in the bell than just the big one that runs from the waist through the lip. In 1975, scientists took a radiograph of the Liberty Bell. A radiograph is similar to an image produced with X-rays. The radiograph showed several cracks along the top of the bell, as well as a crack in the clapper.

FACTS ABOUT THE LIBERTY BELL

he Liberty Bell weighs 2,080 pounds and measures 12 feet around the lip, which is the lowest portion of the bell. The *circumference* around the crown, which is the top of the bell, is seven feet six inches. The bell measures three feet from the lip to the crown.

Other measurements of the Liberty Bell include its thickness—three inches at the lip and 1.25 inches at the crown. The length of the clapper is three feet two inches; it weighs 44.5 pounds. The *yoke* weighs 200 pounds and its wood is Slippery Elm.

The cost of the first bell, which the Assembly of Pennsylvania ordered from the Whitechapel Foundry in

England, was 150 pounds, 13 shillings, and eight pence. Pass and Stow charged the Pennsylvania Assembly 36 pounds, four shillings, and eight pence for their services to recast the bell.

In 1816 the State House in Philadelphia was slated for demolition. But the citizens of Philadelphia stepped in and raised $70,000 to help the city government buy the building, along with its bell. During the *renovation* of the building, the bell was offered to a scrap dealer for $400. The dealer turned down the city's offer, believing the bell wasn't worth that much.

Today, Independence Hall is back in the hands of the federal government. The building is part of Independence National Historical Park and is owned and maintained by the National Park Service. The city, however, still owns the Liberty Bell.

When the bell was first cast by Whitechapel, Thomas Lester, the master founder, used mostly copper and tin. When Pass and Stow melted down the bell for re-casting, they added more copper. But other metals were obviously mixed in as well. An analysis of the Liberty Bell's metal shows the composition to be about 70 percent copper, 25 percent tin, 2 percent lead and 1 percent zinc. There are also very small amounts of arsenic, silver, gold, magnesium, nickel, and *antimony* in the bell.

> About 1.5 million people visit the Liberty Bell in Philadelphia each year.

In 1950, the U.S. Treasury Department and several

At midnight on January 1, 1976, more than 50,000 people watched as the Liberty Bell was moved out of Independence Hall to a nearby steel-and-glass pavilion. Independence Hall can be seen in the background of this photograph of the pavilion. A project to build a new home for the bell on Independence Mall in Philadelphia began in 2001.

private companies commissioned a foundry in Annecy-le-Vieux, France, to cast 54 full-size replicas of the Liberty Bell. The bells were intended as gifts to each state and U.S. territory. They are to be displayed and rung on special occasions. Even though the real Liberty Bell is located in Pennsylvania, that state did receive one of the replicas. The Pennsylvania replica was placed in a shrine in the basement of Zion's Reformed United Church of Christ in Allentown, the location of the Liberty Bell's hiding place during the American Revolution. Other replicas of the Liberty Bell are on display in Tokyo, Japan; Prague, Czech Republic; and Tel Aviv, Israel.

Since July 8, 1776, when it rang to celebrate the signing of the Declaration of Independence, the Liberty Bell has been an important American symbol of freedom.

A SYMBOL OF FREEDOM

ollowing the War of 1812, Americans finally rid themselves of the threat posed by the British, and started addressing the troubles at home. Among those troubles was slavery. In the years leading up to the Civil War, the *abolitionist* movement gained strength. Abolitionists were people who believed slavery was wrong, and they intended to put an end to it.

In 1839, a group of Boston abolitionists known as "Friends of Freedom" circulated a pamphlet calling for the end of slavery. The front of the pamphlet featured a drawing of the Independence Hall bell over the caption, "Liberty Bell." The abolitionists were obviously taking the message on the bell—"Proclaim Liberty throughout all the Land"—to mean all inhabitants of the United States, whether they were free men or slaves.

The publication of that Friends of Freedom pamphlet is believed to be the first time anyone had referred to the bell as the "Liberty Bell."

In 1861, Americans would fight the Civil War to free the slaves. The Liberty Bell had become a symbol of freedom for all Americans—especially those held in *bondage* in the southern states.

But there is no question that the bell first earned its place as a symbol of American liberty on July 8, 1776.

Four days earlier, the Declaration of Independence had been *adopted* by the Continental Congress in the State House in Philadelphia. Following its adoption, the declaration was sent to a printer to produce copies. They were distributed to a number of people the next day, but most Americans were sill unaware that their government had announced independence from England.

On July 6, leaders of the government met again and decided to announce that the declaration had been signed. At some point on July 8, probably at about 11 o'clock in the morning, the great bell in the State House steeple started pealing, calling citizens of Philadelphia to the public square for what was sure to be an important announcement.

Of course, the people of Philadelphia had known the declaration was forthcoming—the Continental Congress

Christopher Marshall, a Philadelphian who saw John Nixon read the Declaration of Independence from the State House on July 8, 1776, later wrote in his diary: "There were bonfires, ringing bells, with other great demonstrations of joy upon the unanimity and agreement of the declaration."

had been meeting for weeks. So when the bell in the State House steeple began to chime, there was little doubt in the city that morning as to what would be announced. Hundreds of citizens flocked to the public square.

Just past noon on July 8, 1776, Colonel John Nixon, an officer in the Continental Army, strode out of the State House, scaled the steps of a platform in the courtyard, and read the Declaration of Independence to the American people. When he finished, the crowd cheered loudly, and above them the great bell in the steeple of the State House announced that America was now a free and independent nation.

1736 The Pennsylvania State House, later to be known as Independence Hall, is completed in Philadelphia.

1751 On November 1, Pennsylvania Assembly Speaker Isaac Norris commissions Whitechapel Foundry in England to produce a bell for the new steeple of the State House.

1752 The bell arrives in Philadelphia in September; it cracks on its first ring.

1753 Philadelphia metal workers John Pass and John Stow re-cast the bell twice; in June, the bell is hung in the Pennsylvania State House.

1776 The bell tolls for the first reading of the Declaration of Independence on July 8.

1777 The bell is removed from the State House steeple in September, and hidden from the British in Allentown.

1824 The Pennsylvania State House is renamed Independence Hall.

1835 The bell is believed to have cracked on July 8 while tolling to announce the death of United States Chief Justice John Marshall.

1839 A pamphlet produced by Boston Abolitionists first identifies the bell as the "Liberty Bell."

1846 The bell rings for the final time on February 22, tolling to mark the birthday of George Washington.

1944 The sound of the Liberty Bell is broadcast to all parts of France as Allied forces land on D-Day, June 6, intending to liberate the country from Nazi control.

1976 The bell is moved out of Independence Hall in Philadelphia to the nearby Liberty Bell Pavilion on January 1.

2001 Work begins on a new home for the Liberty Bell, part of a major renovation to Philadelphia's Independence Mall.

abolitionist—prior to the Civil War, an American who called for an end of slavery.

adopt—to vote to accept something, such as a committee's decision or a proposed law.

agenda—a formal list of things to be done at a meeting.

ammunition—items such as bullets that are shot from a weapon such as a gun.

antimony—a toxic crystalline chemical element. Its metallic form is silver-white and brittle.

assembly—the governing body of a state, composed of representatives elected by the people. Also called a legislature in some states.

bondage—the condition of being enslaved.

caretaker—a person who takes care of a building or object.

cast—An impression formed by pouring molten material, especially metal, into a mold and letting it solidify, so that it takes on the shape of the mold.

circumference—the measurement of the outer boundary of a circle.

clapper—the part of the bell that dangles inside, making noise when it strikes the walls of the bell.

commemorate—to honor the memory of someone or something.

concave—an inward curve.

curfew—a law requiring people to be in their homes and off the streets, usually at a set time each night and signaled to begin by the chiming of a bell.

foundry—place where metal is cast into tools, bells, or other useful objects.

liberty—freedom from control or oppression by another entity.

melodic—having a pleasing sound.

peal—sound made by bells.

prophecy—a prediction of the future.

province—in colonial America, the territory under control of a king or ruler.

renovate—to restore something, such as a building, to good condition.

skirmish—a brief battle that is a small part of a larger war.

solemn—serious or grave.

steeple—tower of a meeting hall, church or other building housing a bell.

yoke— a wooden support frame from which a bell is hung.

FURTHER READING

Binns, Tristan Boyer. *The Liberty Bell*. Portsmouth, N.H.: Heinemann Library, 2001.

Boland, Charles Michael. *Ring in the Jubilee. The Epic of America's Liberty Bell*. Riverside, Conn.: The Chatham Press, 1973.

Hall-Quest, Olga. *The Bell that Rang for Freedom*. New York: E. P. Dutton and Co. 1965.

Riley, Edward M., *Starting America: The Story of Independence Hall*. Gettysburg, Pa.: Thomas Publications, 1996.

Sakurai, Gail. *The Liberty Bell*. New York: Children's Press, 1996.

Steen, Sandra and Susan Steen. *Independence Hall*. Englewood Cliffs, N.J.: Silver Burdett Press, 1994.

INTERNET RESOURCES

The Liberty Bell

http://www.ushistory.org/libertybell/
http://www.nps.gov/inde/liberty-bell.html
http://www.libertybellmuseum.com/
http://www.nps.gov/inde/visit.html

History of the Declaration of Independence

http://www.archives.gov/historical-docs/document.html
http://www.loc.gov/exhibits/declara/declara1.html
http://www.ushistory.org/declaration/

PICTURE CREDITS

page
3:      Corbis
8:      Independence National Historical
        Park, Philadelphia
14:     Ted Spiegel/Corbis
18:     Independence National Historical
        Park, Philadelphia
24:     Hulton/Archive
26:     Independence National Historical
        Park, Philadelphia
28:     Independence National Historical
        Park, Philadelphia
29:     Independence National Historical
        Park, Philadelphia

30:     Independence National Historical
        Park, Philadelphia
33:     Independence National Historical
        Park, Philadelphia
34:     Courtesy © Eastman Kodak
        Company
37:     Independence National Historical
        Park, Philadelphia
38:     Hulton/Archive
41:     North Wind Picture Archives

Cover photos: Hulton/Archive; (inset) Bettmann/Corbis ; (back) Corbis

BARRY MORENO has been librarian and historian at the Ellis Island Immigration Museum and the Statue of Liberty National Monument since 1988. He is the author of *The Statue of Liberty Encyclopedia*, which was published by Simon and Schuster in October 2000. He is a native of Los Angeles, California. After graduation from California State University at Los Angeles, where he earned a degree in history, he joined the National Park Service as a seasonal park ranger at the Statue of Liberty; he eventually became the monument's librarian. In his spare time, Barry enjoys reading, writing, and studying foreign languages and grammar. His biography has been included in *Who's Who Among Hispanic Americans*, *The Directory of National Park Service Historians*, *Who's Who in America*, and *The Directory of American Scholars*.

HAL MARCOVITZ is a journalist for *The Morning Call*, a newspaper based in Allentown, Pennsylvania. He has written more than 20 books for young readers. He lives in Chalfont, Pennsylvania, with his wife, Gail, and their daughters, Ashley and Michelle.